Where's The Title?

Written by
Cherry Selvaggio &
Leanna Selvaggio – Boulalas

ISBN: 978-1-990420-26-9

LABWORKS PUBLISHING

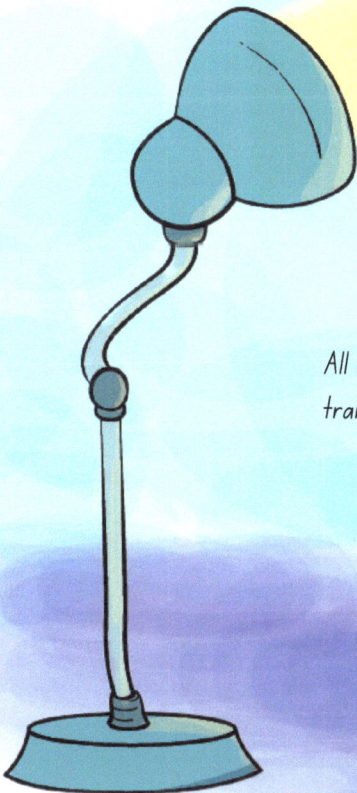

You can call me Mr. Sharpen,

Mr. Creative,

or Mr. Storyteller. Just joking! Let's keep it simple— call me Pencil.

I Love
Writing!

I am so grateful you are here, Eraser. Without you, all my mistakes would be visible. Erase this, please.
Sure!
Wait, never mind. Remove all that instead.
Really? I find it great.

But lately, I've noticed Eraser doesn't always carry a smile.
He doesn't bounce across the page like before.
Something is not right.

WHAT SHOULD I DO?

SHOULD I SAY HOW I'M FEELING OUT LOUD?

SHOULD I KEEP IT TO MYSELF AND JUST KEEP ERASING?

SHOULD I TRY TO FIND ANOTHER WAY TO BE PART OF THE STORY?

SHOULD I BE WORRIED PENCIL WON'T BE MY FRIEND IF I TELL HIM HOW I'M FEELING?

CAN YOU HELP ME DECIDE?

Yes, I wanted to say something before, but I wasn't sure if you would understand.
You can share your ideas with me anytime.

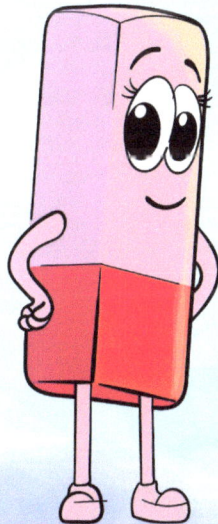

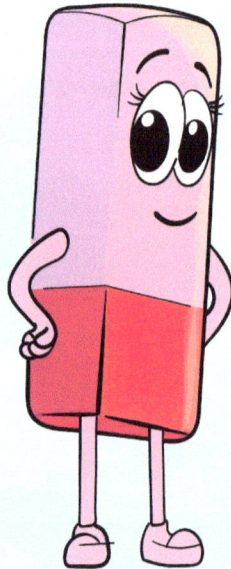

Ideas are unique. They come in many forms and take different directions. It's your story. It's special.
Well, this one is our story.

Let's Discuss Together

We loved having you in our story.
Now it's your turn to share!

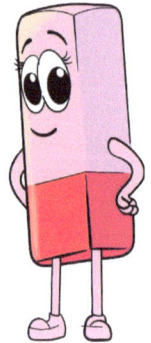

1. What title did you come up with for our story?

2. What makes someone a good friend?

3. What does teamwork mean to you?

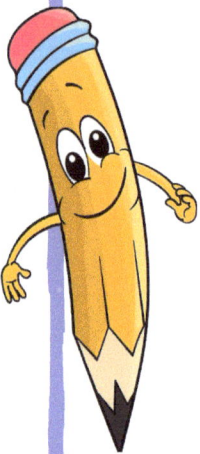

4. Have you ever found it hard to share your feelings?

Let's Learn About Emotions

1- Point to the images below that describe the emotion (anxious/ sad/ happy)

2- Describe a moment when you were anxious, sad, happy

3- Share ideas of what can help you feel better when you are anxious or sad

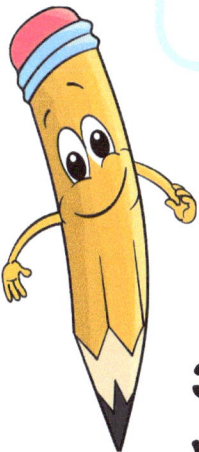

www.ingramcontent.com/pod-product-compliance
Lightning Source LLC
Chambersburg PA
CBHW042110040426
42448CB00002B/210